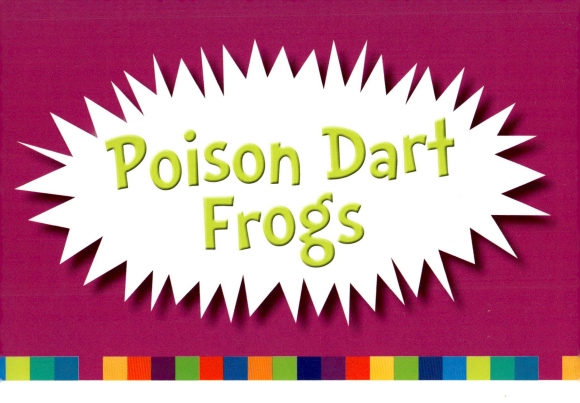

Poison Dart Frogs

BY ELIZABETH RAUM

AMICUS HIGH INTEREST ✦ AMICUS INK

Amicus High Interest and Amicus Ink are imprints of Amicus
P.O. Box 1329, Mankato, MN 56002
www.amicuspublishing.us

Library of Congress Cataloging-in-Publication Data
Raum, Elizabeth, author.
 Poison dart frogs / by Elizabeth Raum.
    pages cm. – (Poisonous animals)
 Audience: K to grade 3.
 Includes bibliographical references and index.
 ISBN 978-1-60753-787-8 (library binding)
 ISBN 1-60753-787-7 (library binding)
 ISBN 978-1-60753-886-8 (ebook)
 ISBN 978-1-68152-038-4 (paperback)
"This photo-illustrated book for elementary readers describes
the venomous poison dart frog. Readers learn how these
rainforest frogs use venom to as a protection against predators.
Also explains how people have used the poison for hunting
and medicines"—Provided by publisher.
1. Dendrobatidae–Juvenile literature. 2. Frogs–Juvenile
literature. 3. Children's questions and answers. [1. Poison
frogs.] I. Title.
 QL668.E233R38 2016
 597.8'77–dc23
                                        2014033279

Editor: Wendy Dieker
Series Designer: Kathleen Petelinsek
Book Designer: Heather Dreisbach
Photo Researcher: Derek Brown

Photo Credits: Alamy/blickwinkel 10; Alamy/imageBROKER
9; Alamy/Jacques Jangoux 27; Alamy/Ken Koskela Cover;
Alamy/mauritius images GmbH 13; Alamy/Stephen Kelly
5; Alamy/WILDLIFE GmbH 22; Corbis/Jim Zuckerman
19; Corbis/Mark Moffett/Minden Pictures 6; Corbis/Piotr
Naskrecki/Minden Pictures 25; Shutterstock/Brandon Alms 28;
Shutterstock/BMJ 21; Superstock/Michael & Patricia Fogden/
Corbis 14; Superstock/Minden Pictures 17

Printed in Malaysia

HC 10 9 8 7 6 5 4 3 2 1
PB 10 9 8 7 6 5 4 3 2 1

Table of Contents

Deadly Frogs

A snake slithers on a tree branch in the rainforest. It is looking for lunch. It sees a tiny frog on a leaf. It gets closer. Suddenly, there is a flash of red. The frog stretches out and shows its colorful body. It's a poison dart frog! This tiny frog is less than 1 inch (2.5 cm) long. But the snake lets it get away. This frog's skin is covered with deadly poison.

Poison dart frogs are small.
Some of the biggest are only
2 inches (5 cm) long.

A hunter blows darts out of a tube. The darts are covered in frog poison.

The Choco people live in South America. They named the frogs "poison dart frogs." The name stuck. Choco hunters use waxy leaves to catch a frog. Then they rub **blow darts** on the frog's skin. The frog's poison makes the darts deadly. Hunters use the darts to kill birds and small animals that they eat.

Not all poison dart frogs have the same poison. Some poisons are stronger than others. The Choco people use the golden poison dart frog for hunting. It is the strongest. It is strong enough to kill large mammals. The poison kills deer, wild boars, and even jaguars.

 Can the golden dart frog's poison kill people?

This small golden dart frog's poison is very strong.

 Yes! A tiny bit can kill a grown man.

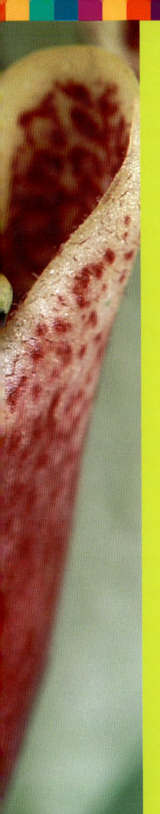

In nature, bright colors are a warning. They tell others to stay away. Poison dart frogs come in many bright colors. Some are bright blue, red, or green. Some are orange or pink. One **species**, or kind, is yellow with black spots. Frogs with the brightest color have the strongest poison.

Bright colors warn other animals that this frog is poisonous.

A Power Lunch

Poison dart frogs do not use their poison to hunt. They have other skills. Their sharp eyes spot **prey**. Their long sticky tongues flick out and catch it. Tasty! Any small bug will do. Poison dart frogs eat ants, mites, and tiny spiders. Small flies and beetles are part of their diet, too.

Bugs stick to a frog's
long sticky tongue.

Beetles in the frog's diet might be what makes it poisonous.

 **Q** Are poison dart frogs in zoos poisonous?

A frog's diet gives it energy. But some of what they eat is what makes the poison. Some ants and beetles have poisons in their bodies. The poison doesn't hurt the frogs. But it collects over time. Soon it seeps out through the frogs' skin.

No. In zoos they eat fruit flies and crickets that do not have poison. Frogs lose the poison when their diet changes.

Using Poison

Poison dart frogs have only one **predator**, the fire-bellied snake. It eats poison dart frogs. The snake's saliva, or spit, makes the poison harmless. The poison does not hurt the snakes. But other kinds of snakes stay away. So do birds. For them, eating poison dart frogs is deadly.

The fire-bellied snake is the frog's only predator.

What if an animal tries to eat a poison dart frog? It spits it out. The frog tastes bad. But spitting the frog out does not help. It is too late. The poison has begun working. It **paralyzes** the animal's muscles. Then the poison attacks the animal's heart. The heart stops beating. The animal dies.

Birds fly over the trees looking for food. But they won't eat poison dart frogs.

Rainforest Life

There are more than 100 different species of poison dart frogs. They live in tropical rainforests. Most of them live in Central and South America. One species lives in Hawaii. They all have strong back legs for jumping and climbing. Some live in the trees. Others live on the ground.

 How did poison dart frogs get to Hawaii?

Steamy, wet rainforests make good homes for poison dart frogs.

 People brought them there in 1932 to get rid of bugs.

Some frogs lay eggs on a leaf.
A parent stays to guard them.

During the rainy season, male frogs look for mates. Each species has its own call or trill. Males trill to attract females. They **mate**. Then the female lays eggs on a leaf or inside a tree hole. One parent stays with the eggs to care for them. Sometimes both parents do.

The eggs become tadpoles in about two weeks. At that time, the mother or father sits in the nest. Tadpoles wiggle onto the parent's back. They ride piggyback to a small stream or pool. Then they swim away. Tadpoles eat **algae** or bits of leaves. In about 3 months, they are full-grown.

 Are the babies poisonous?

A frog carries her tadpoles to water where they will grow.

 No. They are not poisonous until they begin eating ants and beetles.

Frogs in Danger

People are causing problems for poison dart frogs. They cut down trees in the rainforests. They build roads, drill for oil, and dig mines. This destroys the frogs' **habitat**, or home. Farmers are hurting frogs too. Bugs eat farmers' crops, so they use poisons to kill bugs. Now there are not enough bugs left for the frogs. Without food, the frogs starve.

People burn trees to make room
for farmland. This destroys
the frogs' home.

This frog's poison might be helpful. Scientists could make medicine from it.

 Q These medicines are made of poison! Are they safe?

Frog poisons kill. But they can be helpful, too. Companies that make medicines study the poisons in their labs. They want to find new uses for them. Some frog poisons help people with heart problems. Others help with pain. Scientists hope to find more ways to use frog poison to help sick people.

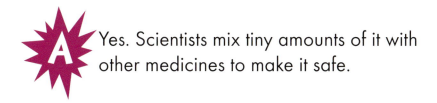
Yes. Scientists mix tiny amounts of it with other medicines to make it safe.

Glossary

algae Tiny plants that live in water or on wet ground.

blow darts A dart that is blown through a hollow tube, making a simple weapon.

habitat The place where an animal is usually found and makes a home.

mate To come together to create offspring.

paralyze To make a person or animal unable to move or feel all or part of the body.

predator An animal that hunts another for food.

prey An animal that is hunted for food.

rainforest A warm, tropical forest that gets lots of rain.

species A kind or group of animals that share certain characteristics.

Read More

Dussling, Jennifer. *Deadly Poison Dart Frogs.* New York: Bearport, 2009.

Kingston, Anna. *The Life Cycle of a Poison Dart Frog.* New York: Gareth Stevens, 2011.

Owings, Lisa. *Poison Dart Frogs.* Minneapolis: Bellwether Media, 2012.

Websites

Blue Poison Frog | San Diego Zoo Kids
kids.sandiegozoo.org/animals/amphibians/blue-poison-frog

Poison Dart Frog | National Geographic Kids
kids.nationalgeographic.com/animals/poison-dart-frog.html

Poison Dart Frogs Games & Videos
www.learninggamesforkids.com/animal_and_nature_games/amphibian-games/frog-games/video-poison-dart-frogs.html

Every effort has been made to ensure that these websites are appropriate for children. However, because of the nature of the Internet, it is impossible to guarantee that these sites will remain active indefinitely or that their contents will not be altered.

Index

About the Author

Elizabeth Raum has worked as a teacher, librarian, and writer. She enjoyed doing research and learning about poisonous animals, but she hopes never to find any of them near her house! Visit her website at: www.elizabethraum.net.